Rendezvous with customers

What wins but hides

C Madhavi & C Rajgopalachary

Secrets and whispers

- Customer is promised business best and Customer is the most promising source of business leadership with àgility, purpose and style of managing market expectations, company costs and consumer attitudes.

Don't open up Customer

- Let Customer enhance the power of silence and secret joy of buying a new business solution for betterment against other customers and curiosity should not kill but have new business experiments with new customer needs to get new user groups.

Don't force Customer

- To understand your business products, you understand Customer
- To be a buyer, you have to want your products
- To give feedback, let your products gel with customers
- To connect with different customers, you connect with competitors.

Prefer

- Customer privacy to company confidential program
- Clean communication to diabetic smile with customers
- Greeting to grating of Customer message
- Agility to reading between the lines
- Collaborative merger to superiority over Customer.

Let Customer

- Think about complex demand for challenging your employees
- Decide price
- Enhance your business credibility
- Enjoy the business offering
- Say no to bad business experience

Toggling between customers and market

- Market is full of competitors and their customer who may turn to your business with or without inclinations to yet another competitor

Customer conducts business

- The business formalises the right offering as conducted by everyone at Customer community and employees should not think that they are doing favour on your business by Customer research and patronage.

Most business changes

- Point to customer for finding a new business opportunity but if you want true and everlasting patron in customer then it may turn you to offer something to buyer as Customer opportunity instead of business opportunity.

Customer opportunity

- It's better than the intended company offering worth in customer ability to fulfill something in life by way of business offering beyond the intended use.

Try to be customer

- Trust in the new provider and try to buy the product to understand what goes into the whole experience of working with sellers and users of products.

Up above

- The world of companies is below that of consumer that's underneath the global community development as a balance race between business and community to get even with customers.

Clenching finances

- Finance is like hands enabling course desired by top management of strategic business expansion but when clenching is likely to hit in customer demands by business control strategy if not managed better.
- The more you control your initial investment the more you narrow return opportunities.

Wins but hides

- Intention of genuine services in the Customer integration of community interest with business effort can grow success without ostentation or exaggerated competition
- A customer like company always wins.

Hides but wins

- Knowledge management
- Information technology and business intelligence
- Informal measures to protect Customer against the global company costs
- Analysis of your customers to understand what you would like to sell.

Loses but wins

- My example of Maggie providing discount vouchers for all regular customers from losing them to rivals due to hygiene safety saga, has led Nestle to success by failure.
- Responsible company can win even after losing to customer welfare.

Trigger wins

- Customer is easy winner in the ability of business to make win that even a discount is considered by Customer as a win following which loyalties and references flow steady to get multiple new business wins with (Customer uses different brands) or against other companies (e.g. Customer is using all appliances of Samsung).

Missing user links

- KYC documents
- Considering the needs of Customer alone gives narrow scope but some data of family and friends can grow closer clarity on the full flow of needs in the user circles to simplify your business attempts on customised Innovation (innovastomise)

Real talk

- Company is in the habit of communicating with customers indirectly from social networks or email or phone in specific time of closing issues
- No business is keen on getting into a talk with customers for business discussion which if done gives consumers a sense of esteem to stay connected by products in your business.

Count the chickens

- Customer is aware of the limitations in strengths of self, bosses should have some information about that of company, both sides must bring best method of fulfillment by guidelines and implementation to multiply their eggs in the different baskets.

Don't break the eggs

- Customer dreams are like eggs that should not be broken in business trying to get them true.
- But the dreams can grow into new hiring, better products, improvement of business performance and even more employees.

User wants product, not company

- Products that you want to stay in customer basket should have clear picture of business changes with the effort to get them made for Customer, not for showing company skills but understanding.

Company wants users and products

- The double sided need of competition wanting both products and users with either as driver, some products drive users to buy or other users prompt the manufacture of products, so that Companies are in need of more favorable attention of buyers who can grow without either.

Market wants buyer and seller

- The rendezvous with market is not possible without buyers and sellers, both sides forming forward measures and methods of promoting needbased products in means and results of business performance in change driven market economies.

Volatilities pump in

- Rivalries
- Switching loyalties
- Reversing Innovation
- Failing Strategies
- Winning coincidences
- Submissive leaders
- Leading followers

One-to-one Customer

- Meeting can grow fruitful insight
- Phone talk can get better customer focus
- Interaction in email, social networks or blogs can open Customer beyond fear
- But sometimes company has to deal without the customer.

Multiple rivals

- Customer struggle in preserving personal instincts and culture is best done by ignoring Companies that innovate because they got investment but not because they got Customer who is going to be taken care of by competition that will pay beyond bounds of return.

Business links

- Connect Customer with results without blaming Customer or employees on the market generated circumstance that goes by sentiments changing business process and product drivers besides levels of time and education in customer direction.

  Understanding Customer as key

Educated Customer

- Is demanding unexpected or more challenging goals
- Is dealing with intelligence and emotions
- Is designed to be part of business changes
- Is logical but receptive to discuss several types of ideas

Existential threat

- What is your threat could be competitor's opportunity and vice versa but rivals exist in customer indirectly of bringing up unexpected request or exaggerated complaint or feedback to Business discomfort with your future scope of strategic discussion with customer.

Training tempers of employees

- The business and markets including user representatives should not deter trust in customer by deviating from Customer concerns towards business contributions, they have to learn to listen more of Customers without reaction in normal human temper.

Mending technical formalities

- Customer is in no position to be told that the company policies and practices are not allowed to hear out or help him, in allotted time or never.
- Culture your machine and employees to identify with customers and rewarding formalities in favour of user or seller security need to be taken.

Rinse Strategic research

- With a focus on main course of Customer interaction whether positive or negative train your resource networks to be free from restrictions of business performance defects, bias or other failed attempts on trying to understand what is acceptable for new customer or change movements.

Rely upon user complaints

- Don't try to get rid of the complaints in business globally gaining the most of Innovation with exceptional solutions for Customer issues as they bring out better needs than business as usual approach because both business and Customer are not aware of some unknown needs of themselves.

Glean Customer feedback

- Look forward to Innovation clues, Customer frustration signals, technology and employees' failure to pay proper attention to Customer as smart rivals may take your customer if you are not giving more positive news for your future business ventures around Customer.

Value buyer criticism

- Don't tell Customer to team up with your business competitors when buyers compare and criticise, but take details of poor experience without any conditions of business, to better their expectations and meet them.

Use technology to bridge gap

- Don't let Customer miss out on experience due to machinist breed of business products
- Enable the process of Customer support even for non loyal customers or users of rivals' products or otherwise to show how much you can win using technology and tools.

Design company culture

- Imbibe Customer emotions, heritage, values
- Include market reactions or adverse events
- Take corrective control strategy against competitive mistakes
- Add critical analysis feedback from employees
- Design business culture as identity and conditions where your customer comfort is your responsibility.

Bring out Customer

- Everything should be done by the company to highlight the best of Customer in different forms though they're small, to illustrate, the food products company could ask for new recipes from Customer and reward each entry with a certificate or voucher or discount or other gifts.

Product is

- No customer responsibility for any inconvenience but Business representatives should have to replace product at regular intervals for new products without any loopholes by depending on the best companies to work like them to wait for your customer complaints to interact with them.

Brittle bets

- Thinking that rivals are waiting to fail for you, or, trying to understand market and not Customer, is no easy feat to get the right results from business centric to be in open Strategy for managing signals from market for Customer service with complete value chain focused aim.

Read market

- Analyse and interpret market by customer review
- Devise business products improving the market and its sentiment pulled by business gaps or Customers' demands for any direction in growth or challenge with changes taking up new shapes in companies, Customers and economy.

Don't misinterpret market

- Utilise the best technologies and business brains to understand what markets say but some mistakes occur due to lack of attention on grounds of business markets in following the simple trends for analysis by junior manager.

Torment of business

- Market can confuse competition beyond bounds
- Cultural differences can call off Business
- Best skills can get outdated
- Leaders can become failure with no notice

Customer review of worth

- One of the customer rights is not feedback at the end but up-to-date suggestions at every stage of business changes that are talking leadership and worth of Customer in propitiation of advanced gains or other forms of satisfaction on management of risk and compliance with customers to make important than buysell relationship.

Go with the best methods

- Customer is no provider of company operations or Strategy but cultural skills to get the best technologies fail not without general impression on the mere machine unless covered by Customer commitment including social values and culture tang.

Product is not

- Product is not pride of Customer but company in showing strong capabilities
- Product is not profit source of business but Customers who want to add value to life and gain by paying less than received.

Customer is secret

- Don't make movie on Customer but respect the privacy of Customer who is your secret resolution because business changes are not predictable in the market so if you let Customer think without revealing everything a good innovation by intuition may be more beneficial than otherwise.

Product proximity

- Customer is in business proximity of your products as much as predicted for your competitors at the same time unless covered by advanced customisation offers more lucrative than others

Initiatives and commitments

- Product or project management yield results for your business initiatives
- Customer experience seeks services to help customers achieve results in giving positive solutions for your business credibility that could compare to your business employee commitment.

Technology adds

- Hiperformance benchmark and tactics of business with globalisation in business solutions that go into future foundation for industry standards led by top quality innovation and competition.

Main menu

- Customer sees family benefit to using product as main menu with the customer service as dessert
- Employees see Customer need as main menu
- Competition sees trouble with rivals to be main.

Business pole

- Customer is a common business pole standing in different locations for different products with a new demand grooming competitors from lifting up new market standards to adding Innovative value.

Hi-tech ventures

- Learn from animals e.g. drones trailing birds, blockchain to be taken after the herd
- Lead laser or Blu-ray or other forms of energy display and conversion
- Like array of Customer demands to pushing business limits on the fact of Customer satisfaction.

Higreen ventures

- Customer is no easy with Technology along which are needed the best value systems specific to product but could bring in better social change at unit usage level of home experience and general acceptance by market level growth of your customers on the regional or international level.

Derived drivers

- Current customers and business representatives are not blaming the market but not blindly adopting robotics at the same time that are driven by mistake or change or challenges or volatilities.

Tactical technology

- Relies on collection of human inputs and Strategy to get credible outputs instead of losing relevance in automation of calculation of Customer preferences by analysis of business products.

Capped capabilities

- Technology is not without conditions or constraints
- Resources are totally dependent upon if
- Ideas generate under favorable environmental situations
- Market is unconditionally conditional or volatile.

Benefits from collaboration

- Cultural values and less competitive advantage to take the form of business changes in the long term profitable opportunities because anyway it's not rivals but Customer who experiences your business products or offers.

The technology valve

- Please let Customer enhance usage experience or understanding of technology before making them include technology in their way of promoting a good need or solving problems.

A tete

- Demanding Customer is more important than project because Customer will continue to get new customer but projects will not get new project without success of existing one (whether project or Customers).

Conditioning

- Customers also care for culture convergence in using your products demanded by them for meeting their non cultural needs
- Business is motivated by advanced market followership and informed interference of knowledge stakeholders.

Nevertheless

- Competition colludes in the process of avoiding overcommitment or extra service to customer
- Company is in negligence of Customer in the name of policy limitations or hierarchy constraints.

Need is the direct input

- First input on business transition is no other feed but the need for business customisation based on the need of Customer in future output of providing specific solutions for meeting customers' expectations.

Need is the output

- Of corrections and efforts on the existing business outputs
- From the customer brainstorming
- For your business ventures in future
- Of competition loopholes

Opt for improvements

- New innovation is taking more challenging inputs from Customer and technology with a solid base of business research in order to change faster with your market signals or collaboration.

Value can

- Company is well off with social networks for your customer references beyond a good product promotion but not sure of Business satisfaction guaranteed by advanced technology value.

Better the bets

- Improve the quality and utilisation within your business products that are watching buyer who is not averse of market competitors globally from positive point in adding their offerings in better discovery of better alternatives in keeping up with their needs.

Depend upon Customer

- In return for your skill of business products accept Customer feedback for new change initiatives in opening new opportunities for they have direct application of your products in their activities.

Feed upon Technology

- Rip it up to see what the Technology can do for you or go after a short term technology update matching that pace around market and knowledge of customer in return for motivation to employees.

Add

- Value of business to different ways of improving consumption
- A win for win and employees are not going to return without creating a good Customer victory

Building brand product

- Business brand equity or Customer growth can grow faster from your competitors accepting defeat by investment in the business process collaboration in growing products that are of global strategic excellence benchmark.

Customers build

- Rapporteur in business competitors to follow Customers with their knowledge and method of further communication and management over expectations in getting global market growth that doesn't compromise on user prosperity.

Take the order

- Of corrections and efforts from your competitors
- Of products and solutions from your customer
- Of lies and management strategies from your market signals because no business is completely ethical.

Unintended

- Consequences come from negligence of Customer
- Innovation can grow benefits from collaboration in the business and user
- Experience can affect the process and growth of technology when Customer and employee are in jitter of difference between idea and understanding.

Customers can get done

- Reviews of business competitors
- Updation of business products
- Evaluation of market sentiments
- Evasion of business changes
- Innovation of modern ages

Little technology can

- Analyse limitless data
- Enable information accuracy
- Derive wonders with customers
- Collapse under pressure of bureaucracy when not managed better

NIB

- Business strategy is a pen writing in future Business offerings in better sharpness of Customer as nib redirecting the ink or resources to get multiple outputs to buyer delight as preparation of business leadership.

Customer journey

- Starts with a new solid dream need
- Traverses multiple refinements with Companies
- Agrees on middle path of business abilities
- Ends with a new product accepted but not expected initially
- Restarts at different companies with modification of dream need
- This is how business exists.

Customers need not

- Say enough but company should show collaborative initiatives in understanding the hidden interest of customer and bringing out solutions for cultural competency and employee compatibility with customers.

User ironies

- Most experiences and mistakes are discounted for few or other new business fit instead of losing product or technology innovations over minor loopholes or other unrelated factors affecting your customers but they could move to rivals for no reason at market surprise.

Boundaries of failure

- Customers fail when they are not able to fulfill cultural or exaggerated competitive selection criteria on pulling new grounds for failure of business enterprises more for Customer partnership than participation in failure.

Expertise instead of

- Competitive imitation is not better option of business changes brought for new quick response by forgoing quality and analysis both of which can supply value supporting the customer along the challenges of market, the process and chain change can be managed better by expertise instead of copying Strategy.

User won't

- Tell about complex innovation provided by the competition
- Think of innovative solutions unless they are supplied by your business initiatives
- Compare turnover of business to select one of your products.

Play with market

- Company is free to experiment with market signals when Customer is not just buyer but global partner in business to different companies that market leadership of user and not ways of competition or corporate abilities.

Building user experiences

- Expectations guide Customer in comparison and company with any direction changes in the process of establishing a new window of experience as personalised interference and offering worth more competitive selection that goes along development of business leadership.

Technology nods

- Yes to all their implementation related improvement solutions in community value enhancement instead of one aim of getting manpower related efficiency

Better to buy

- Seller has better results with future readiness to buy ideas, best practices, greenovation (green innovation) from Customer, Companies or community inspired by change brought in business globally for selling products better than others.

Tent in

- Business as Strategy for your skill and time cultivation of Customer development through technology that goes along new ideas for selling products that help customers with their inconvenience of daily rigor.

Utilised

- Resources are available again with experience
- Technology should be maintained well for future exploitation
- Knowledge is no different than creating multi dimensional opportunities.

Temporary adaptation

- Technology embodiment in the business mission is not for showing alternative dependency but ad-hoc means of fulfillment of business goals for unthinkable innovation in the process of establishing solutions for Customer need.

Best output

- Is that Customer delight of sigh without doubt from using your products which can never win over by irrationality but trust with value based business changes brought in favour of Customer.

Tempering response

- Competition should condition their response by Customer perception instead of rash hasty aggressive Strategy of opposition or support from greed of profit with customers.

Shouts

- Should come from Customer
- Should arise as Technology suffocates the process and involvement of business interaction with customers
- Should complete market signals in altering organisation structure towards Customer growth.

Ambient business

- Don't trouble Customer with your business worries and fears
- Encourage Customer to pay attention to your business changes instead of ignoring against competitors and market collapses.

Buyer is intelligent

- Customers also have experience with new ideas for technology innovation like your expert employees who can grow trained Strategic response against other odds of rivalry tactics and global market challenges.

Don't wait for

- Customers to invite you for turning real their dreams
- Buyer to criticize your business against competitors
- Users to determine alternative solutions for your future business growth.

Render

- Cultural adaptation of business products in high differentiation by Customer expectations because they deserve to be unique outputs despite claiming independence and adherence of traditional values.

Strong in

- Strategic planning and community collaboration can grow you to offer free space for spontaneous innovation but as helpful trust offering more value of quality products and solutions by Customer commitment of employees.

Dress your business

- With attitudes of trust and attachment
- With attention of competition or market
- With delight and inspiration of users
- With sheen of esteem and confidence of buyer.

Wholehearted

Thank you